The ups & downs of GARDENING

The ups & downs of GARDENING

Tony Husband

ARCTURUS

ARCTURUS

This edition published in 2017 by Arcturus Publishing Limited
26/27 Bickels Yard, 151–153 Bermondsey Street,
London SE1 3HA

ISBN: 978-1-78428-752-8
AD005675UK

Printed in China

INTRODUCTION

I love my garden: I love sitting in it; I enjoy all the scents and colours, the bird song and especially the rustling of small creatures hidden in the undergrowth just going about their business. Indeed there's nothing quite like one of those balmy English summer evenings when I'm sitting out there in the cool air with my bottle of Rioja, savouring the scene around me. It is truly one of the joys of life. That's what gardeners are always striving for: being in that moment.

But to get there takes hours and hours of love, devotion and, to be honest, backbreaking toil because, like painting the Forth Bridge, once you get to the end, you immediately find you're back at the beginning, and you have to start all over again. As all gardeners know, gardens never stop growing and spreading – upwards, outwards, sideways and in every direction you can think of – it never ceases. That's Nature.

You discover, the very moment you've pulled out that last weed and you walk back to the house for a well-earned cuppa and a warm bath – at this point, you almost forget your back is aching and your fingernails are crammed with dirt – new weeds have suddenly sprung up out of nowhere already. It's not their fault; it's just what they do.

Of course it's not just weeds that grow; there's also the grass on your lawn, the ivy on your walls, the roses in their beds! And if you don't keep them all under control, they'll rapidly turn your nice garden in your quiet suburban cul-de-sac into a micro version of the Amazon rainforest.

Hopefully some of the cartoons in this book will ring bells with you and not just blue ones. Oh, did I mention slugs?

Tony Husband

'It's amazing what you can teach a border collie to do.'

'For heaven's sake, stop admiring your new shed and get to bed.'

'Your cat keeps doing its business in my garden.'

Florist
'Say It With Flowers'

'Do you have a bunch that says, "Get out of that lazy bed, and sort
the garden out so we can grow our own?"'

'I've had a brilliant idea: let's turn our garden into a vineyard.'

'You're right. Next door has pinched some of our garden.'

'Ssshh! Gardeners' Question Time is on.'

'I'm sure Isaac Newton didn't use that sort of language.'

'Do you want to see my tree house?'

'I don't care if my garden's on an ancient pagan site,
you're not dancing naked on my lawn at full moon.'

'You promised no long names of flowers, Peter.'

'Tom, can we ask what you're spraying in your garden?'

'You're right. It is a mole hill.'

'I told you that creeper needed cutting back.'

'It's a lawn moower.'

'Hello, sir, what's the problem?'

'You've been drinking in your shed again, haven't you?'

'Actually, that lovely silver pattern is slug trails.'

'The stage? Oh, didn't I tell you we're having a rock concert
at the bottom of the garden?!'

'They play havoc with my wind chimes.'

'Stay out of the wild garden!!'

'Funny how some birds get more out of the birdbath.'

'So you're determined to find someone who's handy with
a hedge-cutter and a strimmer?!'

'How come your grass is always greener?'

'Just to let you know, I'm converting my garden into a pay and display car park.'

'Surely, it's my turn now!!'

'We're great, thanks. Tom's happy now he's invented a
remote control lawnmower.'

'Your scarecrow isn't working.'

'That flipping weed's back.'

41

'Come and see how much better our garden looks than next door's.'

'How many times have I told him to fix this flipping fence?'

'You're at it again. You talk more to those damn plants
than you do to anyone in the family.'

'Here's Johnny!!!!'

'Can we get rid of that flipping catmint?!!'

'How many insects find their home in an English country garden?'

'Can you call back? He's on mole-watch duty.'

'So you've been watering this for months and nothing has grown...
Sir, you're supposed to plant things in it.'

'Oh, he's always digging up old bones in the garden.'

'Here's to plastic grass... the future!'

'My plan is to let the weeds grow very thick and wild,
then build a maze.'

'This mole problem's getting worse.'

'I told you the window box was too heavy.'

'The rain never stops... I'm thinking of growing rice.'

'Can't you just buy fertilizer from a garden centre like everyone else?!'

'You come in my garden one more time and it's...'

'Here comes that smart alec squirrel again.'

'We've been invited to Sadie and Roger's for Sunday lunch, and could we bring gardening gloves to help them with their weeding?'

'Here's to a night of fine nettle wine grown locally in my garden.'

'I honestly don't know what I did before I discovered gardening.'

'Hello, Molly. As you can see, I've a fantastic crop of mistletoe this year.'

'How, erm, novel... hanging–basket earrings.'

'Hello, yes... my husband wants to complain about the hover mower you sold him.'

'Watch yourself, Tom. A couple of my deadly poisonous snakes have escaped.'

'I knew it. He wasn't building an allotment down here.
He's dug a tunnel to the pub.'

'Oh, there's all sorts in the pond.'

'You're right. They are giraffes. I need to sort out that garden.'

'What is it?' 'It's a flower bed, silly.'

'Our grandchildren are in there somewhere.'

'There was a bee in that rose you sent me.'

'No, he's out tonight guarding his prize marrows.'

'Yes, the garden is full of weeds, but I like weeds.'

'Harvey, have you electrified the birdbath again?'

'I've got a pretty big garden. Do you have a lawnmower with satnav?'

'Make sure you don't go sniffing that. It'll see you off.'

'Can I call you back? I think Robert's struck oil.'

'It's about your Leylandii...'

'He wants to be buried in his allotment between the strawberries and the carrots.'

'Hello, I'm Arthur. Do you know, I could tell you the Latin names of every indigenous plant in Britain.'

'Hello, Missus. Want any crazy paving putting down?'

'It's not been the success you'd hoped for, has it, dear?'

'He really has got something against that gnome.'

'I'll be glad when the lawnmower's repaired.'

'I'm expecting a bumper crop of carrots this year. Shall we see how they're getting on?'

'I sincerely hope that's eco-friendly plant spray, Grandad.'

'Okay. Mr Wriggly Worm, go back and do your work.'

'Shouldn't it be green side up?'

'What on earth do you find a gardener to do in such a tiny garden?'

'I wish he cared for me like he does his precious garden.'

'Erm, yes, I suppose the photographs do make the garden look
a tad bigger.'

'That flipping nuclear mole is back again...'

'Oh, good save, Mr Smith.'

'Darling, the doctor says I've developed severe hay fever.
He recommends we concrete over the garden.'

'I've just found those bulbs you promised me you had planted in the bin.'

'I'll give you a tour of our gardens... hang on, I'll get the Land Rover.'

'There's so much blooming rubbish in this garden. It's unbelievable!!'

'You're putting me on gardening leave?! But I don't have a garden.'

'Did you remember to tell your dad about the wasps nest?'

'*Apparently, they don't like visitors.*'

'I've never known a winter like it.'

'Shouldn't the bat box be in the garden?'

'I'm sorry, dear. Stamping on it isn't an option.'

'Your scarecrow's terrifying my kids.'

'That? Oh, it's a nuclear bombproof shelter I had built.'

'Perhaps if you did a little more work in the garden,
and a little less reading about it...'

'No, I've no idea where he could have come from either.'

'These are nice, Carol... Carol... Carol???!!!'

'I told you to sort out our ant problem ages ago.'

'Harry, this is Frank. He likes to waffle on about gardening too.'

'Would you mind sorting your garden out? It's about to invade mine.'

'Damn slugs are attacking the Hosta again.'

'I know the garden needs doing, but what can I do? Some field mice have nested in my wellies. I'm stuck.'

'Don't get me wrong. I love the roof garden; I just didn't expect
its roots to come through the ceiling.'

'I know that sunflowers are meant to be tall, but even so...'

'The people who owned it before had such a lovely garden.'

'I'm looking for effort-free gardening plants.'

'It's another aggressive, invasive species, I'm afraid.'

'These are my daughters, Daisy, Lily and Poppy. My husband's a bit of a gardener.'

'He's building a private members' bar at the bottom of the garden.'

'It's nice to have a friend at the bottom of the garden.'